Foreword by Steve Benne

I knew Roy for many years, initially fro[m] worked there. I also went to The Mission Church for many years and got to know him and his family well. I knew he had written a book of poems that I never purchased. I was also aware he had written this book and I'd never seen a copy. I started looking for a copy and could only find one for sale at £20, when I next looked, I couldn't find any? I thought it was very sad that Roy's future family might not be able to get hold of a copy in the future. The copy I am using belongs to Roy's daughter Linda or I would not have been able to undertake this task. I think it's important that this book can be found by future generations, for the reason below!

I had found a copy of a book by one of my forefathers that had been written in 1774, then after some research found he'd also written a book of poems in 1796. Books were very expensive to get published back then and he had the backing of the Duke and Dutchess of Marlborough and many other benefactors. I've put both of those books into modern day English around 2009, so was aware although its time consuming it can be done.

I have therefore taken the time to transcribe this book for future generations of Roy's family and the people of Rushden. I have copied it down in the same way as Roy wrote it, I don't agree with all the grammar or the use of commas and full stops and I would certainly have put many more question marks had I written it? The main thing is the book is available again for those who want to read or own a copy. The books will be sold through various channels but Lulu.com will have the rights for any sold, I will add an additional £1 on the price to go to the Rushden Mission Church, I know Roy would have liked this, as he devoted many hours to the building.

Authors note

This is the 4th printing of this little book, which both surprises and pleases me. I am obviously pleased that it should be so successful, and surprised that there are still so many people who half remember the Rushden that I knew when I was a boy, and who want to renew the acquaintance. Lik J.R. Hartley in the yellow pages advert, I had no copy of my own, and people were constantly asking where they could obtain a copy, hence this reprint.

It has been pointed out to me that I made several glaring errors in the original, for which I apologise. I did point out, however, that I did no research, and everything was off the cuff and from personal memory. When anyone gets to my age, dates of events are not so important as the events themselves.

The bombing of High St. I now realise, was in 1940, not 1941 as I stated in my early editions. I am fairly reliably informed that the swimming pool was opened by Dr. Greenfield in 1929, not 1926 as I said, although each day when I passed the pool on my way to work, I feel sure the date I noted above the door was 1926.

In my walk along High St. I am told that I omitted the Sketchley Dyers and Cleaners from next door to the Maypole. I am not personally, a pedantic sort of person, but I appreciate that those people who pointed out my errors, were merely trying to forewarn me from attempting histories without research. Perhaps Pepys was sometimes inaccurate, but if he was, I forgive him, as I hope you will me.

Roy Blenco

I hope that is not the case with this offering. Please read on...

FIRST I WAS BORN...........

Where do I begin? What are the first memories of the town in which I was born, in which I was raised, schooled, and finally, (or almost finally) retired?

I suppose that Westbourne Grove is a good place to start, because that is where I started. Number four, to be precise. My grandparents house, where mum and dad, "lived in" as the expression was. If geography of Rushden is not your strong point, Wastbourne Grove was that part of Wellingborough Rd. From the 'Oakley' crossroads toward Oakley Rd. It is now incorporated in Wellingborough Rd. But the house is just the same from the outside.

The railings out to the front gate were the first thing I remember remembering, because the round wrought iron rails were topped with a spade head, and I fancied they were spears, particularly the one that moved in its socket. It may well be that I gathered the idea of spears at a later time in my childhood, but certainly no later than seven, for that is the age I was when grandad died.

We lived as soon as the council housed us, in Irchester Rd. This was a road that began and ended on a hilltop, with a lesser hill in the middle. We lived atop the middle hill.

The bathroom was a cold water only affair, at the northeast corner of the house, and protruding slightly from it's neighbours, to form the beginning of a small crescent. The icicles hanging from the runnels in winter were a sight to behold. The bathroom was not however, a cosy place to bathe. A tin bath in front of the fire, was the normal routine in my formative years.

At the outward end of Irchester Road, on the right, was 'Park Farm', known by all as, "Tubbys'", and the meadow which accomodated the milking herd, doubled as a sportsfield for the Mission Hall. Beside this, or perhaps because of it, it was also an adventure playground for all the children who lived in the road, that is, those of the middle hill and the last hill.

For a start, there was the brook. It was not a brook in the true sense of the description, but a drainage ditch that formed a pond in the field, and the outfall of the pond trickled across a meadow, giving us a 'water world', and the challenge of jumping over it that almost always ended in failure.

Having crossed the stream, to give our shoes time enough to dry before venturing home again, there was, 'playing on the roller'. The Mission Church cricket eleven had their mown patch at the farthest end of the field, and a huge roller to keep a reasonably flat surface. The mere presence of it was a delight to us kids. It could be a bus, or train, or tank or most often, a climbing frame.

Close by was the "Pavilion". This was a wooden hut with a fence around it, whitewashed to make it different from a garden shed. In this hut the cricketers stored their gear, changed into their 'whites', and in the event known as the 'Mission bun fight', which included a childrens sports day, from this hut was dispensed by a lady called Mrs Bandey, Slices of madiera cake and Kali lemonade.

The MISSION CRICKET ELEVEN around 1930

To complete the picture, there was a tennis court. The relatively small Mission Church had a sports field, voluntarily maintained, and used by the numerous teens and twenties of that organisation, to a standard to which a good many villages and a few towns still aspire.

This was the sports field of one small group, in the next field was another area for the use of Dentons cricket club. Two fields away was the field belonging to, or at least used by, St. Peters church, for their sports day.

At the other end of town, in Bedford Rd. Was the well set up sports field of John White Footwear, And in the middle of town Caves factory had its tennis courts, adjacent to the factory. The Park Rd. Baptists had there own facilities and so did a few others. There were two sports parks; Spencer and Jubilee, and a 'Sunday' park, Rushden Hall grounds. In addition to all these was the town football ground and cricket ground, which at least once in the season hosted a first class County cricket match. At this time Rushden had a population of fifteen thousand.

Rushden Swimming pool was born in the same year as myself, 1926, and was supervised by one man, Bill Elliot. During the open season, May to September, it was immaculately kept, both in standards of cleanliness, and in pool discipline. In the closed season, Bill painted the street lamps, every one, every year.

On the subject of streets, these were kept clean, in spite of the predominance of horse transport, by sweeping with a broom, and the resultant dirt was taken away in a handcart. If they were not immaculate, at least the dirt and litter was less than one day old.

The entrance to the old pool, when it first opened.

GRANDFATHERS HOUSE ON THE HILL

I can see the chair, green velvet covered,
And that very large 'Grandfather' clock
A mantelpiece cover, with tassels of silk,
And the clock going- tick- pause –tock.
Bright were the burnished brass 'fire irons',
Always neat was the jarful of spills
That stood in the polished brass fender,
In grandfathers house on the hill.

In grandfathers house, I'd be quiet as a mouse,
'Til grandad came in through the door,
Then he'd catch me and tickle me,
'Til nearly sick I'd be, in a giggly heap on the floor
What a wonderful face he had!
Whiskered, with teeth so bad
They looked like the Avebury stones,
Every bell that was rung,
In which steeple it hung,
He could tell by the depth of its tones.

Every Saturday noon, I would get there too soon
For the Saturday pennies to spend,
The joys that he gave to me, the toys that he made for me,
There wasn't a thing that HE couldn't mend.

To Bellringing practise together we'd go,
And I had my own rope to pull.

Ding, and let go, Dong and let go,
Then up to the bell tower with bells ringing full.

On Sunday, The one day it shouldn't have been,
He'd meet me, and greet me with, "Hey, Sunny Jim"
I'm off to the "Works" to pay for m' coal,
And you can come too if you'd care for a stroll".
Without hesitation the pact there was made
For I knew that the 'coalclub' also sold lemonade
Together we'd stroll, his cane gaily swinging,
To return an hour on, and my heart would be singing.

But there came a grey morning, in the fall of the year
When mother called to his bedside so dear
And we'd not been there long when a voice said,
   "Doll, come"
And she went, and returned, in her eye was a tear........

She tried to explain that he'd gone up to heaven,
But how do you say it to a small boy of seven,
Whose friend is no more?
Close quietly the door
Draw to the plush curtains and make the room dim.
The room was his housekeepers, not part of him.
But the green velvet chairs, and the clock I see still.
In Grandfathers house at the top of the hill.

SCHOOLDAYS ARE THE HAPPIEST?

At the age of four, I started school at the Moor Road infant school. This was about threequarters of a mile from my home, I am quite certain about this, but I think that was the last time I was ever taken to school, for ever after that day I was considered old enough to cope on my own or with friends.

Westfield Avenue had been built by this time, and a number of the children from that street were attending Moor Road, which ought to have meant comradeship, but there was childish hostility between Irchester Rd. and Westfield Ave. and that meant that not only was there no comradeship, but that I had to hurry home to avoid the 'Wessy' kids.

In my own group (of houses) there were boys at the same school, but several years older, which at school is an impenetrable barrier, my next door neighbour of the same age, who for some reason attended Alfred Street school, and my very best friend who was a girl, and attended Newton Road School.

Moor Road School intake class was presided over, in my year, by Mrs Norman a lovely, 'cottage loaf' type of lady, who was about to retire at the end of the year. Her influence on me was so great that she made me want to go to school, when in fact I really hated it. She taught me the first rudiments of phonetic letters, and how to shape them, starting with the lower case. For instance, 'h' was a lady about to cross a bridge, whereas 'n' was merely the bridge.

She must have taught her son Reg. too, for he became locally famous for his poetry, and for his dialect jokes featuring 'Air Ada'.

Miss Hodgkins was the daughter of a local farmer, and she taught the second year at Moor Road.

Now infant school teachers are a breed apart. Everything they say, and everything they do is more truthful than St. Matthew, and once said, can never be unsaid to that trusting, eager child. I listened avidly to every pearl from Miss Hodgkins lips. I remember her reading to us what was purported to be a newsletter for a dog, (whose name escapes me) which was actually from the pen of a young Enid Blyton. I equated Miss Blyton in my childs' mind with Miss Hodgkins, and had I ever met the lady, I would have expected her to look exactly as Miss Hodgkins did. I suppose that at the age of five, I was in love with my very first lady!

The top class at Moor Road was taught by the Head teacher, Miss Scholes, who, after Miss Hodgkins, appeared elderly to me. In later years I was able, in business to serve her, and she still looked, to me, exactly the same age. Miss Scholes taught me something of history, the tree dwellers, the cave dwellers, Stone age, Iron age. These were all introduced to me by this good lady.

I was an apt pupil and enjoyed listening and learning. I was impatient with my classmates when they appeared to be dull of understanding the simplest things. I wanted to read the next paragraph of life before I set the book down....

But I was cockahoop, and just had to be brought down. I contracted meningitis (which at the time was called brain fever) and that put me out of the education race for the remainder of the year.

When I re-started, it was at Alfred Street. Alfred Street School was the biggest one in town. There were ten classes, five in the "A" stream and five in "B". I started in "A" under a worthy lady named Miss Bennett. In the class were twenty five boys and twenty five girls. Within the class there was 'zoning'. If you were not doing very well, you sat near the front, and if you were practically perfect, you sat at the back. I sat somewhere near the middle. The girls were on one side and the boys on the other. Any bad behaviour on the boys part, and the offender had to sit with the girls, (As punishment?). Girls were sugar and spice, and were allowed to leave the class to play, and to go home, first. Boys were-well-not!

The Headmaster, when I first started at the school, was a tyrant and a martinet, whose name was Reid. I remember being taken at sometime, with the school (at our own expense) to see the film 'David Copperfield' in which the hero is maltreated and beaten by a sadistic Mr. Murdstone, and in my childish mind, Murdstone and Reid were one and the same person. The actor who played Mr. Murdstone had a physical resemblance to Mr. Reid and that possibly fostered the illusion, but the sadism was not an illusion. This fellow hated children in general, boys in particular, and loved to hurt people.

I have sometimes been known to advocate bringing back corporal punishment in schools, as a last option, but the thought of that man, and the thought that there could be others like him, stop me before the idea gets any further. Whether or not his bullying behaviour became known, I do not know, but he was replaced by a kindly man, Mr. Sid Lawrence, and school became bearable once again.

Because of my aforementioned affliction of meningitis, some part of my brain seemed to be stopping my hand from functioning. It was as if I was a naturally left-handed person being forced to write with my right hand, and so I became very clumsy, and slow. If anyone as old as I casts their mind back, they will remember the days of steel pens. Pens that of their own volition, rolled off desk tops and became crossed. It didn't matter if your own nib had remained intact for weeks, it always got damaged at the end of a spate of, "My nibs crossed, Miss." And so your pen went unrepaired. The powdery ink didn't help, either.

To make my short story even shorter, my combined unskillfulness with pen and ink, and the crude tools in use, caused me to be transposed from the 'A' to the 'B' stream, just for the scholarship year. The "B" stream were not considered to be suitable material for scholarships. I think, perhaps the teachers were being kind, knowing that some pupils were less than likely to succeed, they tried to soften the blow of failure by not putting them to the test.

The class I moved down to was wonderful. Because there was a shortage of actual rooms, this class was held in the hall, so that everything that was going on could be seen, including the little dramas like, which boy was sent out for misbehaviour, and who had to see the Headmaster.

Most of all, the teacher was great. Her name was Mrs. Levy. Mrs. Levy was a widow, and old enough to have a daughter who was I believe a nurse. She was the one teacher in the whole of the school, who walked home with a flock of her class surrrounding her, chattering away and skipping about her, as if she was a favourite aunt on a rare visit.

In her class, boys and girls were mixed, within two seater desks, and in studies. Everyone learned to sew, sing, and do handicrafts. This I think is common practise now, but it was not the norm then. Brighter pupils taught the less bright to read, and to do arithmetic, etc. In fact, Mrs. Levy was a very free thinker in a very restricted environment.

At the end of the year with her, having come top of the class in my end of term exams, I returned to the higher echolons of education once more, by the simle expedient of changing my pen and ink shackles for a pencil. The really clever things are the simpler ones.

Alfred Street School many years later!

H. E. BATES and others.

In the penultimate class at Alfred St., which in my own case turned out to ultimate, the teacher was one, Miss Nellie Groome, who taught as her main subject, English. Miss Groome had the reputation of being very strict with her class, and so she was, but I thought she was marvellous. She was enthusiastic about her subject, and was able to discuss the details of the classic poets lives. On the wall across the front of the classroom were pictures of dramatists, authors and poets, starting with Shakespeare and ending with Brooke, with a summary of titles of their works.

One important author was not among them. He was important to Miss Groome, because she knew him, and his family. We children were constantly reminded that this was our ultimate goal, in English, to reach the heights attained by the local hero, Rushden born H.E.BATES..

H.E.BATES. we were reliably informed, wrote about local characters so well, that if you knew them, you could easily recognise them, by the accurate description. We would then be given the task or exercise of writing a description of a fellow class member, from which Nellie Groome should be able to identify the subject.

In later years, I read some of H.E.BATES novels, and it is true that the area is taken as a background, 'Love for Lydia' being particularly identifiable, but the characters, I felt were each an amalgam of several well known local people. It was as if he had taken several of these paper dolls, cut them up, and reassembled them with the wrong heads and limbs. But, yes, they were recognisable people, and I acknowledge that he was indeed a great story teller.

My personal preference are his short storied featuring the character, Nat Titlark..

But back to the author. Although he was acknowledged proudly to be Rushden born, he was educated at Kettering, and as soon as he was able, moved to the South of England, the 'Stockbroker belt'. So my honest opinion is that he was not a local author at all, though he may well be the best author who originated in this area. You see, we are thinking about Rushden, the town where I was born, and apart from military service, have lived all my life.

Miss Groome was proud to have known H.E.BATES. I am proud to have known Reg Norman of Rushden, and about Rushden. Reg was quite severely disabled, but ran a one man manufacturing business, and wrote poetry and prose, in both standard English and in the 'kent, shent, wunt, of the local dialect. Now there was a Rushden author.

In those days of long ago, the staple industry, in fact the only industry in Rushden, was the manufacture of boots and shoes. The alternative was to be in the service industries, like shops, banks or offices. The vast majority of school leavers started work in a shoe factory. The best way to, get on, in a shoe factory, we were told, was to learn the trade at the technical school, so this, im my last year at school, is what I did.

In Victoria Road, the Junior Technical School opened its doors for the very first time in, of all years September 1939. The opening did not make the headlines, because some other little matters overseas took precedence. Furthermore, we were a total of twelve scholars.

The school had a different atmosphere to anything I had previously known. It had 'Grammar School' type of status, with a uniform of sorts, and we were treated, at last, as people, rather than as obnoxious brats. For instance, we had mid morning 'Break', instead of 'Playtime'. And we were allowed to stay inside to play table tennis, instead of being herded out into the yard. For the twelve scholars there was a staff of four teachers, two trade and two academic.

Our Science teacher, Mr. Thornton, was a humorist as well as a brilliant teacher (in the manner of Johnny Ball the television presenter of educational programmes), and his little cryptics are with me still.

For example, in physics, he was teaching us about the term, 'Inclined Plane', as follows:-

Q. Why is a sheet of foolscap like a lazy dog?

No one knew.

A. Because a sheet of foolscap is an ink lined plain, an inclined plane is a slope up, and a slow pup is a lazy dog!

Yes of course it's silly, but the fact that I remember the line, even today, means that the method worked.

On another occasion, we were working with acids, alkalines and salts, 'When you mix an acid with an alkaline, the result is salt- which is neutral' he explained. Only seconds later he knocked over a container of salt solution. His immediate response was, 'Ah, well, Neutrals are always getting knocked about'. At the beginning of the war, this was obviously a very topical joke.

STARTING WORK

At this time, most, 'eleven plus', boys had an after school job (or before school, if you were a paper boy). Mine was with the baker and confectioner, Walpole Smith. There was. In fact, no Walpole Smith, but the Walpole part so identified them, that Miss Smith and her brother Fred hyphenated their fathers Christian and surname to differentiate themselves from the memorable Smiths in the town.

Miss Smith was one of those Victorian type of ladies who thought that boys should be hidden from view, except when actually working, or when spoken to. But she was a kindly soul, also, so she would sit four of us boys on the short flight of stairs at the back of the shop and give us scalding tea and 'yesterdays' buns.

To hungry early teenagers, all food is ambrosia, but this was high quality confection that nowadays would probably be sold as fresh. Even today, I can never pass a baker/confectioner's shop without a nostalgic mouth watering.

Bakers of course, delivered warm, fresh, bread daily, except for Sunday, Christmas day and Good Friday. My job was to take a basket of bespoke bread to outlying customers, on the front of my bike. For this I needed a bike. My parents arranged for me to purchase one, a 'COVENTRY EAGLE' from Mr. Espin, in Queen St. This shop is still, at the time of writing dispensing bikes to those boys who need them for their paper rounds, and is still presided over by a Mr. Espin. (I hesitate to call him 'Junior' because he is within hailing distance of my own age) I understand from Mrs. Espin that this shop, with the other, Ross Neville in High Street, are the only shops in town which are still in the same families and still trading in the original business in which they started.

Back once more to the Bakers rounds!

One small round was done in the lunch hour, and a longer round in the evening. On Saturday the whole of the morning and part of the afternoon was taken, for not only was it a double delivery for the boys, but double baking and double delivery for the two employed bakers. The men's delivery was made by means of a handcart.

As I said earlier, no bread was delivered on Good Friday but Hot Cross Buns were, and they were delivered hot, and early, by boys on bikes. When the buns had been delivered, the remainder of the day was a holiday. Although most people worked in factories, they were home on Good Friday, and also the shops and offices were closed, because of the significance of the day. What it meant for bakers, of course, was a double delivery on Thursday and another on Saturday, (which had to cover three days, Monday being a bank holiday).

At the time, a two pound loaf cost 4d, or one and a half new pence. At a very early age, I became aware that a number of people were unable, or unwilling, to pay their bakers bill of around 2/- or ten new pence.

When I mention 'Bespoke' bread, I wish to imply that bread was sorted for people, as individuals. If Mrs. A, for example, wanted a lightly baked 'tin', then that is what she would have delivered. Mrs. B wanted a well done hearth baked 'batch', and that's what she had. Mr. C a crusty 'coburg', Mrs. D a double long tin.......

Eastfields always had four pound steamed tin loaves so that all the inmates had exactly the same sized slice. They were all baked in the same coal fired oven at the same time, but the shape, size, and method of baking varied enormously, and each customer was catered for individually.

After the baking was out, the cakes, pastries, on alternate days, were cooked in the residual heat of the oven.

One baker, Bill Brown (I think) specialised in pastry, and the other, Dick Mitchell, in cakes. Whilst one baking his speciality, the other was out wth the handcart, delivering bread.

Yeast bakery was run in with the bread bake...It wasn't an easy life, nor a fast buck?

This Sylvan scene is a view along Newton Road around a hundred years ago
Photo kindly loaned by Mrs. P. Mole.

GAMES AND CRAZES

It seems that, looking back, the most important thing in childhood was to be in fashion gameswise. Of course, there were the normal ball games, but even they had fashions. Sometimes it would be chucking a 'sorbo' ball at the wall and catching it on it's return. At other times it would be marathon like bouncing sessions, with variations like, between the legas, backwards, etc. Or alternatively, there were games like 'Pig in the middle'. These were all year round standards.

The games that went in cycles were, for instance, 'marbles' and 'fag cards', the latter being a test of skill in floating or flicking a card through the air at a target card, propped up against a wall, and knocking it down. The successful player then won the pool of all the cards floated by the other contestants. The skilled players always seemed to be rich in cards, the lesser ones would have to go back to begging fathers and uncles for cards to replenish their meagre stocks.

Most games were playable in the street or road. 'Cat and stick' was one where a short pointed stick was hit at the point with a longer stick. This shot the small stick in the air, and then it was well and truly whacked. The player who knocked the stick the farthest was the winner. In this game there was no stake to win or lose and therefore it was the most popular one. The actual measure of distance was in paces from the start point, and that was a manhole cover in the middle of the road. It was very safe, on top of the middle hill. One could look for traffic, and if anything appeared in the distance, there was plenty of time to take your turn before the car arrived. If the car was an Austin seven, it was the district nurse, in all probability, anything bigger than that, and it was more likely to be the doctor on a house call. There were, of course, other cars in town, but they could be counted on ones digits if the shoes and socks were removed.

Skipping was another road wide activity. Not for us the individual rope, and the loneliness of the single skipper. Ours was a long, road width, rope, enabling two skippers to be involved at the same time. It could be, and often was, doubled in length and intertwined with a very intricate skipping pattern being executed by the skipper, until he or she was 'out'. In addition there were formal skipping rotation games, where a particular form of words were chanted in rhythm with the steps.

Almost no-one had a formal skipping rope, but somehow. Everyone had the means of this very basic exercise. (A lot of factory bales were roped in those days, I believe.)

"Sheep, sheep, come over", was the name of another game we were able to play across the road, because of it's traffic free condition. In this the person who was 'It' called the players across the road from the far side, and had to capture them as they crossed. The actual rules have become lost to me over the years, but I am quite sure that they were very fair, and made absolute sense to the players.

Hide and seek. This is a world wide game, of course, except that in Rushden it was called, 'HIACKIE', or at least that is what it sounded like. When the hidden person was found, or spotted from a distance, the seeker called out, loudly, "Hiackie Jack one two three, sixty" and that was totally binding. All you had to do was get the words right.

MRS DUNMORE

In the days of childhood, before the war, we had the depression. In Irchester Road there was a shop, a small general store, run by Mrs Dunmore, occasionally helped by her family. The shop was merely the front room of an ordinary house, with a deeper than normal bay window. The shop which opened to eight o'clock every night was an absolute magnet for the numerous kids who lived in the street, that is, the middle hill. None of us had any money, unless someone's mum had bought, for Sunday consumption, a single botte of lemon spruce, and the bottle was redeemable for a halfpenny. That child was fortunate indeed, and the halfpenny was the subject of tremendous speculation, as to what could be brought to give the greatest return on capital. (Poor children are among the best business brains on earth).

I don't know who actually likes aniseed balls, but aniseed balls were the most likely purchase, because a ha'penny yielded ten of them, and they were long lasting. This was a major consideration, when there were so many hungry and friendly mouths to feed. If the crowd was less than five, then one could indulge the palate to the taste of 'Radiance' toffees. If there were seven, then the choice was 'Sharps', a smaller and cheaper toffee, but with ten, well, it just had to be aniseed balls. The alternative was something like cashews, or something that could be divided meticulously, for children are very fair and exact about such things. Mrs Dunmore indulged us. None of us were of the stature to go away on holidays. What we did instead was walk to Ditchford, and picnic and bathe there, the picnic was normally a 'Knobby', that is, the crusty end of a loaf of bread, with butter and jam, or something similar, and a bottle of still lemonade from Ha'penny bag of, 'Kali'.

Part of the equipment for a good day out wax a net made from whatever could be found in the rag bag, on a bit of wire and a jam jar in which to bring home the catch. But Mrs. Dunmore actually went to the seaside for her holidays. Once a year, for a whole week, the area was without her ministry. But never fear, she thought of us in her absence, and brought back for every boy and girl who was ever in her shop, a stick of seaside rock. All the same all pepper-mint, but one for everybody. What a lovely thought. What a lovely person!

SCENES FROM CHILDHOOD 1935

To Dunmores, shopping, we would go
With only half a penny,
Or stand with others in a row,
When we hadn't any.

In that grand, though small, emporium.
Delights were there to buy
And etched as 'in memoriam'
Remembered till I die.

Sherbet dabs, or fountains,
Or barley sugar sticks
Light or dark stripes, mountains
Couldn't make you sick.

Five large 'Radiance' toffees,
(or six of those by 'Sharps')
Could send we kids to heaven
Unaccompanied by harps.

Ten aniseed balls, a ha'penny
Would buy, or four Bullseyes,
Basically identical,
Except, of course, in size.

Then there were the groceries
That mother used to take.

A quarter pound of butter
Weekly for mem'rys' sake

Firewood by the bundle
Unctions by the score
Washing soap and soda
From sacks upon the floor

Polishes by 'Mansion'
Or Ronuk. By the door
Just opposite the crates of pop
Were broomheads. Furthermore

With all those costing pennies
For those whose pay was late
Dear old Mrs Dunmore
Would run a weekly slate

And from her summer holiday,
When she went to the sea,
For every child within her scope
A stick of rock there'd be

I'm sure that if St. Peter,
From looking in should stop,
Then dear old Mrs. Dunmore
Would serve him with some 'pop'.

THE OLD FORGE

One of the seasonal games for which equipment was required was the bowling of hoops, or bells. They were called 'Bells' because of the noise they made when bowled along the highway, being made of wrought iron, and controlled by a stick.

Occasionally these bells would fracture, and when they did they were taken to Billy Ginns, the blacksmith and farrier, to be repaired.

"I haven't time to do that today", he would say, "come back on the first rainy day".

Sure enough, on the first day that looked remotely cloudy, the farrier's shop was inundated with small boys awaiting the services of 'Wag' Lewis, to mend our bells. We didn't mind waiting. The blacksmith shop was a fascinating place to be at any time. The forge was blown by hand bellows, the handle of which was an ash pole capped at the end with a cow horn. When it was worked by the worthy 'Wag', a huge shower of sparks would fly up in the canopy, and 'Wag' would rake through the fire bed to remove the accumulated clinker. I would watch him fascinated, as he fashioned horseshoes from a straight bar of iron, ringing out a tune on the anvil as he did so.

'Wag' had a smoking habit. His pipe started out, I imagine, shaped like any other, but he never used matches to light it. Instead he would fire up the forge with the bellows, pull out a glowing iron and hold it to the pipe. Being right handed, he always held the iron at the same side of his pipe and consequently burned the wooden bowl down at one side.

He was also renowned for not buying tobacco, accepting a pipeful as his 'perk' from farmers and draymen, as and when they required his services. His main grumble was that his working pipe was so burned away that when he was in receipt of this munificence, he could not get enough in to make a decent smoke, or he had to pack it in so firmly, the pipe wouldn't draw.

As I remember him, he was perpetually in a bad temper, and reluctant horses were belaboured with a hammer. This, of course made them even more reluctant the next time they came.

Billy Ginns, son, or grandson, of the original A.T.GINNNS was a little man, nothing like the blacksmith of the song, 'With large and sinewy hands'. He was a locksmith, a pleasant fellow, among whose duties was that of winding up St. Mary's' clock, daily. He was personally responsible for the clock being the correct time and incidentally, for the starting of all the factories.

Inside the door of each factory was the clocking in clock, and alongside was an official document stating that the time was, set and corrected with the clock of St. Mary's' church'. Radio was not unknown at this time, but nor was it commonplace, so the clock, as well as the sermons, was taken as gospel. Of course, the clock chimed each quarter hour, so the blacksmith of Rushden was concerned not only with the boys 'bells', but also with the bells that kept the town in time.

As farming became more mechanised, A.T. Ginns became more 'Agricultural Engineers'. And even transport repairers, with those items that overlapped with smithing, such as road springs, hingebars, etc"

The old smithy kept many wheels turning which would otherwise have been stilled, during the second world war.

Sadly the old forge, and its cottages, are no longer part of the Rushden scene.

From the blacksmith forge, looking south. Foreground, the Coach and Horses, in the tree arch, the Waggon and Horses

A very early photogragh of High Street South, Showing the old "Coach and Horses" and the gates to The Hall. Photo kindly loaned by Mrs P. Mole.

BUTCHERS AND COOKS

Does the French word 'Abbatoir' sound better that the English 'Slaughterhouse'? I suppose it sounds more clinical, and less 'butchery'. But that is what butchers are, or were.

There was, I suppose, a butchers establishment for every house in a radius of about a hundred metres within the town. How they all made a living I will never know. Our local butcher was called Travill and Brown. The (presumed) senior partner, Mr Travill, was a thin, undersized man, and this trait was emphasized by the enormous size of the two Brown brothers. One of these two had 'Prince' for his given name, probably because of his resemblance to the Prince Regent, or because his dad really wanted a dog. I do not remember the names of wither Mr. Travill, nor the other Mr. Brown, but it doesn't matter in this case.

Butchers were people who brought animals at market, slaughtered them, and sold meat from a hanging carcass. No cook worth her reputation would have brought meat already cut and packaged. The butchers own judgement and knowledge of animal anatomy was their stock in trade. Their reputation, either as a good butcher, or as a fair to middling one, rested on this knowledge. Every part of the carcass was used, and the housewife knew the name of each cut of meat, and what she expected it to taste like. If it did not come up to scratch, the butcher lost his customer.

There were, in addition to butchers, vendors of imported meat, like Argentine beef and New Zealand lamb. Pork and poultry were not imported, because they were 'Back yard' products. There were very few families that did not have a few hens at the foot of the yard. People of discerning palate would be disdainful of imported meat, but it was probably better than the best meat available now.

The way meat was cut, as well as the way it was killed and hung, was a major factor in the taste of the resultant meal. This was before universal refrigeration, and everything was fresh. In the same way, 'New laid' eggs were just that. Eggs that were a week old were simply not 'New Laid', and preserved and imported eggs were only used for cooking.

The norm, was to keep a few hens in the backyard, and to eat the eggs daily, as they were laid. When the hens went broody, you did not eat eggs- just the ones preserved to make the Sunday pudding.

However it might be done in Yorkshire, the way Sunday pudding was made in Rushden was with the joint of beef, or lamb, in the middle of the baking tin, and the batter cooked around it. This stems from the time when it was bakehouse pudding, and the baker opened on Sunday morning to bake the dinners that were too big for the domestic cooker. (The oven at the side of the range).

All the ingredients were put in the tin together, carried to the bakehouse, then collected at the alloted time, ready to serve. Often this task was carried out by the father of the family, who was often returning from church, or from the pub, depending on his own particular persuasion. He was usually responsible for the distribution of the meal to the family. I imagine one of the reasons for this domestic chore was to ascertain that he got his share at the right time. No dad, no dinner!

It was not normal practice to use pork in this way, as the meat would not have been cooked. Furthermore, pork butchers were a completely different type of people, being a much specialist cooks as being butchers.

This building was "Masons cottages" The site was used to build the "Victoria Hotel", now "The Rilton"
Photo kindly loaned by Mrs. P. Mole.

FLOCKS FROM FACTORIES

When I was quite young, at least young enough to look forward to an embrace from my dad in the street, I would wait for him to come home from the factory. In those days there was a factory in practically every street, and for the most part, men worked within a few hundred yards of their homes, enabling them to come home to the midday meal, which was always called dinner, and was the big meal of the day.

Indeed, it would have been virtually impossible for him to stay at work for his meal, because there was no provision of things like staff canteens, or rest rooms in which he could have eaten a packed lunch.

I would watch for the factory to disgorge it's workers, and what myriads of them there were. Men would walk up the hill, five abreast, in coutless row upon row, and fifty five minutes later, they would all return, suitably refreshed. There was never any thought of slipping away before the end of the shift, (although it wasn't called a shift), even though they only lived just a few hundred yards from the factory. They would be lighting up pipes and cigarettes, and chattering away about racing, or football, like schoolboys released from the classroom.

The regime in factories was that when you clocked on, you started work, and when you stopped work, you clocked out. There was no time for a chat, and even a visit to the toilet was looked at askance if, in the opinion of the foreman, it was made too frequently. The foreman in those days was not a representative of the workforce to the management, as is so often the case now, but the boss' paid deputy, with the divine right to hire and fire. This put him in a very strong position, and few would argue with him for fear of losing their jobs.

On the positive side, there were so many factories in the area, that (outside the depressed years) there was always another job to go to, in this one industry town.

When father appeared I would run to him, and proudly walk the short distance home by his side. I cannot remember when I stopped this practice, but it must have been well after I started school, and furthermore, I was not alone in doing it, because my schoolfriend's dad worked with mine, and we often met them together. Time softens the sharp edges of memory, so whether we were four, or eight, or somewhere in between, I would not like to say.

As far as I am aware, most of the town was similar, and at the rush hour the roads were crowded with the boot and shoe trade workers walking home. There were a number of buses, and a few people had bikes, if they worked on the 'wrong' side of town, but the feeling was of a happy, busy, 'together', town, run by a council who knew the populace and their needs, because they were OF the town. For example, the wide pavements that are a feature of the council estates of the thirties, reflected the fact of the homeward walk of the factory hand.

The tendency now seems to be to consult the Ministry of Transport, The Police, The Finance Committee, and then to embark on some harebrained scheme that no one wants, and has little to do with the needs of the residents.

Station end of High St. The tall building on the right came to be called, "The Belgian House" The site is now where Kwik Save was?

WHERE DID THOSE NAMES GO?

There was a time when it would have needed no explanation. Anyone in Rushden could tell you, as soon as you asked, the whereabouts of 'Packmans Puzzle'.

It was in fact a labyrinth of terraces which formed and was called, Dell Place. The was no road access to it. A lane led from Newton Road (serving as rear access to Grove Road) to the upper end, and another lane came from the lower end into Park Road, opposite Griffith Street.

Another little terrace of houses could be reached from Griffith Street or be bypassed via the Wheatsheaf Yard, or, in the other direction, access might be gained into Co-op Row, another non street.

Pinch Gut was the name given to that row of houses properly called South Terrace, an alley of tiny houses between Park Road and High Street South. But you couldn't get out at the bottom. (Well, there was a way, but it was a bit of special knowledge).

Another 'Street' in that area was 'Greens Yard'. It was named after the factory that stood at the lower end of the yard, belonging to 'Zoonie' Green, before it became 'Grensons' of Cromwell Road (or the 'Rock') the yard was called 'Albion Place'.

Park Road took its name from the little playing field at its farther end. But that park was built up as a prefab estate following the war. It was once rumoured that it would be the natural extension to the cemetery, but I'm sure the living had a much more valid claim to it.

Mannings Lane once was the very extreme edge of the town in the southerly direction, but it was built upon and called a street, then built beyond, until it is now well with the town bounds.

Off Higham Road was a little group of houses that was a community all of its own. Its proper title was Sussex Place but to all Rushden people it was referred to as 'The Rookery' or even just 'The rook'.

In Bedford Road, every delivery man was aware of a group of houses known to them all as, 'The Golden Staircase'. These were perched on a wall, opposite the 'Compasses' public house. The access to these was by means of a very Steep stairway.

There were alleys in all parts of the town, each having its own little community. I can remember for the Silver Jubilee in 1935, that Orchard Place won an award for the best decorated street. Streets like George Street and Woburn Place, were close communities. Now they are gone forever. Or have they?

Some of these groups still remain, and some have been demolished to make way for new housing sites. They may not all have been Ideal Homes, but they were a characteristic of the old Rushden scene.

THE LENGTHMEN AT RUSHDEN STATION

John, Bert and Henry were length men. They were responsible for the welll being of the five miles of branch line that joined Rushden and Higham Ferrers to the main line to St. Pancras in the south and to the north as far as L.M.S. reached.

Every single item of maintenance was within their scope. They were, collectively, fencing specialists, hedgers, ditchers, harvesters, (with scythes), stonemasons, bricklayers, linemen, pest exterminators, and any other thing that might occur on the length, short of a derailment.

Henry was the foreman. He organised the work schedules for the other two by saying something like, "I reckon we ought to do that bit of hedge today". And the other two would nod in agreement. Then they would gather together the various tools that they would need for the job in prospect, and set off to walk the length to wherever that particular job happened to be located.

Their headquarters was just east of the station, about a mile from the extreme lengths end, and was in the form of a line cabin which contained the tools of the trade(s) and a stove on which a huge kettle of water invariably simmered, and benches on which the three stalwarts could rest between various assignments. It might be assumed that this freedom of thought and self-responsibility would have dulled the motivation to do a good job. It is also true that at 3.30.P.M. on a Friday, the line cabin was usually occupied by the three men, ready to go home. But strangely, all the work that needed to be done on that length was done, and furthermore, these three were often awarded the title and prize for the best kept length.

Bert was not the foreman, nor was he the labourer, but he could be found fulfilling either role, in the absence of the true occupant. He was steady, sage, reliable, and very pleasant in conversation.

By elimination that leaves John. John had a somewhat wry sense of humour, and a lot of muscle which, in that job, he needed. He was also quite accident prone. Normally he would be seen with a plaster or bandage somewhere about his person. This never, as far as I know, stopped him from doing his tasks.

Henry was prone to asthma, and a bit 'hearty' but held down his very responsible job until the length was closed down by Dr. Richard Beeching.

The length is now a wilderness (and rubbish tip), the marshalling yard east of the station is a county council 'area', and the station building itself has been moved back in time to the early part of the 20th Century, being a 'nostalgia' museum.

I am sure that if John, Bert or Henry were alive today, they would be saddened to see the sorry state of the length they so ably maintained. They were not proud men, but their work was something of which to be proud. However, the station, the 'length' and the three men are now part of history.

A view from Wymington Road towards High street South. The building in the arch of trees is the factory of "Zoonie" Green. Albion Place behind the factory was known as 'Greens Yard'. The firm is now 'Grenson's.
Photo kindly loaned by Mrs. P. Mole.

MY WAR

War is one of those tragedies of human existence, along with plagues and famine, but war, in retrospect, could have always been avoided. Having established that war is a horror, it has, nevertheless, it's lighter movements.

I was thirteen years old when the 1939-45 war was declared. Old enough to be scared witless at the thought of the imminent calamity, and young enough to be, well, ditto. My entire teenage was spent in war conditions, or conversely, my whole war was spent as a teenager.

Moonlight, that romantic heavenly light for lovers, was made less enchanting by the fact that it was also a bombers' moon. In this environment, we youngsters had our entertainments, The Ritz, the Palace, and the Royal Theatre, our local cinemas, were open every night, and were full, or nearly so for every performance.

There was a hall, known at the time as St. Peters Hall, in Highfield Road, later to become St. Marks Church, and in this hall were held the Saturday dances. We either danced to, or eyed up the 'talent' by, musical quartet known as the

StanGeorgians. what are now called groups were in those days called dancebands. As I recall Stan was one member and George (Bayes) was another. The pianist was Alan Bathurst and there was A.N. Other. Instrumentally it comprised of a piano, string bass, trumpet, and drums, and we experts of the time, being familiar with such greats as Dorsey, Goodman, Herman and the rest, rated this combo pretty highly.

Quite a number of (now) elderly married couples made their first acquaintance with each other at those dances at St. Peters. Sadly, quite a number who lived and loved those early romantic years did not survive the war that they bravely went and fought.

Other dances were held at various halls in the town, factory canteens being a typical venue. John Whites in Lime St. Eatons in Gordon St., and the CO-OP hall (I think) were used in this way. We seemed to have lots of things to do, but little time to do them and no money to spend, either.

Everyone who was still a civilian was more than fully employed but no one had any money to spend. Public houses were not the main attraction of teenagers, although we didn't avoid them. By and large, pubs were for older people and of course, if you were over eighteen you were in uniform, and entitled to go anywhere.

I was in uniform in 1944, and very soon after that the Germans gave up the struggle.

Somehow, just after the war was a lot worse than the war itself. We were conditioned to 'live for the moment, 'cos it may be the last one', but suddenly we were safe, bankrupt as a nation, and had all the mess to clear up.

This with Stafford Cripps austerity drive, was a bit as if we had a wild party, and had woken up the next day to find that we had all the washing up and housework to do. the war had been no party, but there was a certain euphoria which had to be lived through, to be understood. Even now, fifty years on, people still gather for those nostalgic, 'Forties' nights, either to remember lost friends, or their own lost youth. We were after all, a part of great world history. We revel in the memory of 'congas' in the church hall, the mates we had in the forces, and so on, but we forget so soon the blackout, the air raids, the rationing, the shortages, and the lost friends and loved ones.

Yet every November, people who are possibly too young to remember, gather to day 'Lest we Forget'.

WE 'BABES' OF THE TWENTIES, NEVER WILL!

YOUNG DREAMS IN THE WAR

Down to the wharf, we walked.
And the bright moon shone around,
Occasionally we talked,
Conscious of every sound
We stood and viewed the moon,
Reflected in the stream,
Our hearts in rhythmic tune,
As I told you of my dream.

The ruined house of stone
That stood back from the quay
Would be our future home
And workplace. You and me
Would build a tearoom there,
And There'd be boats for hire
We'd have the finest fare,
And a great, big, open fire.

Under a bombers moon
The siren began to wail,
Spoiling out lovely tune,
We returned along the trail,
And the cold and frosty air
Made us shiver and shudder more
Than many another pair
Of youngsters, in the war.

RUSHDEN AND THE WAR

It may come as a surprise to readers of this history, but Rushden was invaded several times during the war.

The first time, as far as I can remember, was in 1939-40ish, by a contingent of Canadian soldiers, who were the nearest creatures to Americans we had ever seen, apart from on film. They were nice blokes, with a transatlantic accent that we could understand, and not boastful, but with a friendly manner. Rushden liked them, and because they were the first, Rushden had not yet got fed up with service men.

They were not here long. Just a few weeks, It seemed then their place was taken by the 15th/19th Hussars. There was also a laundry, but that may have been part of the same unit. The vehicles were mainly Bren gun carriers. These were tracked vehicles, like a tank, but open topped like a cistern, so that gunner had an all round field of vision, and so that anyone lobbing a grenade could kill the entire crew with no bother. Still, they looked the part. I remember we also had some part of the Royal Horse Artillery among us.

These British soldiers were in various niches of the town. The Windmill Hall housed quite a number, for instance.

The aerodrome at Chelveston and a dispersal field at Podington were manned, at first, by the R.A.F., but when the USA came into the war, these bases were occupied by the U.S.A.A.F., much to the delight of many of the local girls, who seemed to think that they all lived within a hundred yards of their own favourite film star, if indeed they were not filmstars themselves. They were by our local standards, very well off, both in goods like "Nylons", chocolates, "Candies", etc. And the amount of money they were paid, and were able to spend locally.

To be fair, it wasn't just the girls who benefited from these affluent and generous Americans. Lots of the local businesses boosted their earnings by selling things like bikes, cars and services to them. We all benefited from their bravery in flying bombing missions over German, and losing many of their number in doing so.

Another invasion was quite early in the war, and this was by the evacuees from the Walthamstow area of London. The war hadn't really started yet, and all it meant to us was a bit of chaos in the schools. It was a bit more traumatic for the poor kids who had been wrenched from home. This was in the days of the "phoney" war. Unfortunately, when the bombing started in 1940, families in real distress from Stoke Newington were glad to be here. And we were glad to be of some help.

We were their refuge from the bombs, but we didn't escape completely, ourselves. We were hit by a lone raider from the Lufwaffe in, I think, 1941, and one stick of bombs did quite a lot of damage, and claimed several lives. It was a cloudy day in the morning, I recall, and it was rumoured that the bombs were merely jettisoned, not aimed. If that is so, the German pilot was remarkably fortunate in hitting his target.

He hit the Victoria Hotel, at a point about twenty yards from the railway bridge. He demolidhed the fishshop of Bates, in the High St. And a row of houses in West Steet. He hit Caves factory in College Stret killing some of the workforce, and worst of all, he hit the Alfred St. School, killing and injuring some of the children. There were also, if reports were true, unexploded bombs in Church St. And St. Marys Ave. Whether or not I have travelled in the right direction in describing this, I don't know, but that is the direction I walked when I left the factory in Spencer Road.

The gas masks that we each carried seemed rather inadequate to cope with the sort of destruction we were witness to.

We had one more "incident" as the quaintly described air raids at the time. It was at the time of the Blitz on the City of Coventry, a series of nightime raids, which must have been devastating. Just one heavy bomb fell on Robert St. causing heavy damage and a number of deaths. One person, who is a well known businessman in Rushden, was at the time, orphaned for the second time, losing his adoptive parents in the raid.

Being a night raid made it all seem so much worse. we could hear the ominous drone of the planes flying over, and the squeal of the bombs as they fell through the air. We were all very frightened, or stupid, or liars.

We were able to see the B47s, or Flying Fortresses rendevous over the area before setting out on their daylight raids over Germany, and we saw the cripples limping back, and we wondered if anyone that we knew, personally, had failed to return.

Although, when I was in the army. I was sent in that part of the country called at the time, "bomb alley", and we were subject to bombing by V1s and V2 missiles, I was never as upset as I was by those two isolated raids on my home town.

I was, and am still in love with Rushden, and I vowed whilst I was travelling the world with the army, that when my service days were over, I would never live in any other town. And, if I couldn't work in Rushden, I wouldn't work! Fortunately, I was gainfully employed every day from leaving school at fourteen, to retirement at sixtyfive.

It is not a boast, but I am rather proud of my record of fiftyone years of full employment, even though a lot of it has been low paid, dirty, labouring type of jobs. I think I was born at the right time of the century to have plenty of work, and I was also a Saturday's child, which, according to the rhyme, "works hard for a living"......

Roy and Jean's 65th Wedding Anniversary on 31st January 2015, I added this picture whilst retyping and printing this book, to ensure future copies remained for Rushden and the family in the future.

THE BUNNY RUN

In my early teens, it was the done thing to inhabit the 'bunny run' each Saturday evening, that is, to walk the entire length of the High St. From Wills' corner to the Royal Theatre, and back and forth, and back again, in the hope of encountering some girls with whom to spend the evening at the 'Picture's.

There was a figure in that parade who was constant every week, his pitch was at the corner of College Street and High Street outside the 'Rose and Crown' where, as likely as not , the Salvation Army Band was conducting an open air service, people were queuing for the Ritz, and shop workers were making their way home after a tiring day. This was a teenaged lad, on a pair of those old fashioned crutches, with a huge pile of 'Football Telegraphs' known then as now, as the 'pink un'.

Whatever the weather, he would be there, never seeming to catch colds as did we lesser mortals, always a cheery smile for all his customers. His name was Fred Hales. When later on, he started up a greengrocery and fruiterers business, his manner assured him of eventual success, and he was soon able to move into a better shop. Years afterwards, when he might have taken things a bit easy, Fred still had his pitch outside the 'Rose and Crown' because, as he said, he still enjoyed keeping in touch with his past, and he wasn't ashamed of his start in the business world.

When I think back over the years, it seems that every person who ran a small business in Rushden was not just a person, but a personality. They were good at their chosen job, and proud of it, and they had enough enterprise to make a go of it. Furthermore, they didn't encroach on anyone else's trade.

The supermarkets of today have wiped out the specialist purveyors that were once the life of a small town. Strangely, even 'general' stores seem to have specialised in being just that.

One particular tradesman comes to mind as I write this. On our hill in Irchester road we kids used to wait, in the afternoon, for the appearance in the distance, of a blue and white box tricycle, loaded with Walls ices. It was ridden, or pushed, by a gentleman called Harry Green. We would all four of us run to the bottom of the hill to make sure he would be able to manage the climb, and to help him push his burden up the slope. I feel sure, in retrospect, that he would have managed to push it much better without us, but he would smile at us and share between us one penny ice pole, as a reward for our help. Occasionally we were able to buy from him, but over all I believe he must have been out of pocket. Later on he became an ice cream man in his own business, and he had a pony cart from which to dispense his wares. By this time we were teenagers and we could buy from him, but unfortunately the war stopped the manufacture of ice cream. And that was that.

When did we reach the peak? At what precise moment did we start to run downhill? I suppose that the discipline and the shortages of wartime caused a reaction. I certainly seem to have lived in two different eras. I am aware that nostalgia sheds a rosy glow over the past, but somehow, It's not JUST nostalgia.

I spent my teenage and early twenties in the army, and I look back with disgust at those years, though I don't suppose it was all bad. My childhood was not the lap of luxury. I remember (just) the hungry thirties, and yet this was a good time in the town of Rushden.

It was a town of pleasant walks, clean streets, tidy and used parks, and virtually crime free. Even the childish crime of 'scrumping' was looked on as an offence and, if the offender was caught, he was severely punished. Corporal punishment in schools ensured good behaviour (at least in the presence of adults), and people such as park keepers, and cinema commissionaires, were second only to the police as the ultimate deterrent.

We did not feel threatened, simply because we were aware that these people existed and we behaved accordingly. Yes of course there were rebels. But they too, knew that if they were caught, they would be dealt with. And it would be no good complaining to dad about it, for his punishment was likely to be even more severe, and in addition.

We did not ride our bikes on the pavement. (If we had bikes), nor did we ride them without lights after dark. We did not help ourselves to cake, sweets or fruit from home unless we were told we might. Although this by todays standards, may seem petty and mean, at that time it would have meant that you had stolen someone else's share of a special treat. It just simply, was not done!

This, then, was the style of life in Rushden I remember.

Fred Hales who sold the 'pink un' on his crutches, this was his shop at 196 Wellingborough Road. Picture courtesy of Rushden Museum

HARRY GREEN

I remember Harry Green,
An ice cream 'Man of note',
He started with a tricycle,
But later had a float.

We'd meet him at the bottom
And help him at the top,
He'd share between the four of us
A 'Snowfruit' lollipop.

I think he was a Yorkshireman,
(He may have been from Lancs)
To whom, or where he came from,
I'd like to give my thanks.

His 'High Class Icecream Parlour'
(The first I ever saw)
Had just been newly opened,
When closed down by the war.

I don't know where he went to,
I only know he's gone,
And poor old Mrs. Harry Green
Just couldn't carry on.

But if he's with St. Peter,
I'm sure it's very nice
To leave off playing harps and things
To eat a chocolate ice........

WORKING AFTER THE WAR

When I was demobbed from the army, after a few months of trying to settle down in the trade of vehicle mechanic, I threw away all my training and became a coalman.

I worked for the Rushden CO-OP. The CO-OP in Rushden employed around two hundred people. The society had its own bakery in Newton Road, and their bread was second to none. It was delivered fresh daily, by an army of full time delivery men. The milkmen carried out a similar service in the early mornings, and at a guess, half the people of Rushden took this service. The other half was shared by a number of independent bakers and dairymen.

At the CO-OP we had five coal delivery lorries (whose original drivers must have been Ham and Shem, ref; Genesis) and we all loaded at the same time, assisting each other under the hand and eye of Bill King, the coal foreman.

But King was a real 'character', and his capacity for telling stories was simply phenomenal. Even when the tale he was unfolding had been told and heard several times, he could still make it fascinating to hear. Some of my happy memories of this unglamorous job were on those very wet mornings, when it was not possible to go outside, and we would sit in the coal office, listening to Bill's anecdotes regarding his old boss, one Charlie Adams, (of Souldrop, who was probably H.E.Bates model for Nat Titlark).

His opposite number in the private coal trade was Dick Barrett, and the names that these two called each other on these occasions was a separate education.

Coal bags are, (or were) weighed upon the lorries, on a balance, Coal was lifted or shovelled into the bags through a doorway in the side of the railway wagon. When the bag was almost full, it was lifted onto the balance, which put it out of view of the loader, who then had to rely on instructions from the bagger.

The make weights all had different names according to their size, and we were all expected to know them.

"How much does it want?"
"A good bit."

"That it?"

"A touch more...... that wasn't a touch, that was only a snuff! Go on...... Another snuff."

"That's too b....... much, I said a snuff!"
This conversation was virtually unending during all the loading periods, and all the bags had to be correct, as they were subject to spot checks by the weights and measures authority, and they could not be overweight, because coal was rationed at the time.
After a few years, I left the CO-OP, and went to work for the idependant firm of W.A.Scholes. This was a bit like changing from working in a factory and going to a bespoke bootmaker. Each customers particular requirements were individually dealt with they were categorised and committed to memory, as to how they liked their coal stacked in the barn, whether they ordered in plenty of time, or at the last minute? Did they demand best coal? Or cheap coal? Or large lumps? Or cobbles? Did they have a bunker or a

barn? Or boards at the door, and was there barrow access?

Apart from the occasional complaints about the quality of the coal itself (which with natural products it is difficult to do much about) I never, in almost twenty years, heard any complaints about the service. Notwithstanding, however, within three years of tapping of North Sea Gas, I was out looking for a job!

During my time as a coalman, I must have delivered to every street in Rushden, (and every Cul De Sac.) It was extremely hard, anywhere in town, for a house to be locked, or barred in any way. In fact, I was often amazed that on a council estate, the rentbook, complete with the rent money, was often left on the front doorstep, probably alongside the insurance premium. And the milk money. Such was the honesty and trust that prevailed at the time.

I am not delving into history, except that it is in the past, this is our town of twenty five years ago.

It seems very sad that now, if I walk a hundred yards to the shop, I have to lock all doors and windows, because of the prevalence of crime.........

TOMMY ESSAM

In those far off days of the youth of the writer, three names were household words. This was before television and fame or notoriety had to be earned. The famous three were Charlie Chaplin, Cloddy King and Tommy Essam.

Charlie Chaplin needs no explanation, so how about Cloddy? Well, he ws the butt of all those jokey stories, some funny, some disparaging, which nowadays have the name Paddy in them. This was in the days when an Irishman was simply someone who came from Ireland.

Tommy Essam was a completely real and local person. He was a showman, or 'Carnie'. His main source of fame was an electrically illuminated tombola, contained in a circular stall. Very modern in the days when a good many people in Rushden had gas, or even oil, as their first choice of lighting.

In the centre of this stall was a roundabout of two peacocks in full plumage, one with a fan on it's breast, which helped to give the illusion that it was electrically driven.

The rotation of the device activated a rotary multiple switch, which in turn lit up a series of place names. Tickets were sold to the punters, and where the prize light stopped, then that ticket won a major prize. The ticket had on it two place names, so after the winner had given up his ticket, the rest of the punters had another chance to the second prize.

Tommy took his machine to all the local fairs- probably all those named on the prize board, but when the season came to an end in the Autumn, he had a small fair of his own, on the site where the Ritz cinema/Bingo now stands. When the site was taken to build the Ritz, he moved to the site which is now the car park adjacent to Arbuckles.

Tommy was quite a generous man, but very astute. He always gave good prizes of value to his punters. This way, he kept them coming. He also gave to the inevitable gang of boys that frequented his fair, enough toffees to fill their school caps, and occasional free tickets to his stall.

Many local people, now in their seventies and eighties proudly say that such and such a treasured possession, such as a clock, a tea service, or a dressed doll, was won for tuppence, from Tommy Essam's!

I cannot say with any certainty that Tommy was a religious man, but on his main stall was a notice which read,

'God helps he who helps himself— But God help him who helps himself here!'

In spite of his apparent generosity, I repeat that Tommy was an astute businessman. Had he carried the same stock in a High Street shop, his sales might have amounted to say, one dozen sales per day. In the sales method he used, however, he could first of all sell manufacturers seconds, that is, cups with slight flaws, etc. without the risk of people returning them for a refund, (for how can you return something you won as a prize). Secondly, he sold a fairly major item of household ware every five minutes.

He always had a crowd around his sales area, and all he needed to sell were tickets, not goods, the giving of free goes to the children ensured a start to the crowd, and the goodwill of the parent of the children. The number of tickets sold was carefully calculated to cover the retail price of the prizes and, in theory, everyone was a winner. Everyone, that is, who won. The punter who, as in every prizedraw, brought the non winning ticket, simply paid for somebody else's prize. I feel quite sure that they did so willingly and would never- not even now, after all these years- hear a word against Tommy Essam, Rushdens Showman.

Tommy Essam's Steam Engine with Tommy in the picture.

SPIT ROCK

"Ayer bin feaust yit, Gel?"

"Whirr! Tent nuthin likea feaust, not like w'ustevisist. Theyent nuthin there!"

"Whirr, thamusta bin summut thee lars night, else we ennarf spenta lot on nuthin."

"Yis, buddit ent thsairm, thrent no feaustballs, unthrent no spitrock, n' nuthun. Its all that pickin dam straws, un that. Y'kent roll pennies cus theyent bigganuff t'roll, 'n y'gotta spenda quid t'git harfacrown cokernut, Tent wutha light!"

"Whirr, yu kent expect it ter be th'sairme us wot it were wen you wurra gel, or else thed still be steamorsis n' stuff."

They want nuthin th matter wi' steamorsis, unorgans, un cokernut shies. Least yuccud chairse round arter blokes wiya feaustball, unevva bituv is spit rock, aura bite orf is toffeeapple."

"Un yuccud goo in the 'walludeath', ifya want frit to, but I cou'nt never goo cus owwa allus frit t'death attit."

"Thrent nuthin like that now, The dawnt git gooin till they comeout the pubs, Un then its all fightin, yortodum thother night!"

"Yuh, onnow, but theyenall like it, sunny them wot dorno n'betta, Tent fair on thothers."

"No, N' ospose its cheaper t'goo pubbin th'n feaust.

Yatta payya quid t'goo on anythin like th'dodgems, n' thrent no sideshows likethwere, like boxin, n' walladeath t' keep yu out the rairn furra foo minutes."

"Yuh! Un dornit allus rairn fa Ruzden feaust. Well! Om bin ear fruvva sixty year unomunny known one wot ent bin wet, yit."

"Omm still goddarfa teaset orf Tomy Essams wot owwunfa tuppence, yudornatta tell me owoldyare owwa in yore clarssut school. Under ol' 'Buggy'."

"They weree good dairs, or praps wiwwa a bit younger then."

"Yis, gel, ospose yuright, well, oslatta goo, tada."

"Tada, gel, remember me t'Bert, wuncha."

RUSHDEN FEAST

There always seemed to be an apt saying for any occasion, like, for instance, "When you can hear the trains at Irchester, you can be sure of rain?" I don't suppose this applies any more, because of traffic noise, or "Ghetto blasters", or even that trains are less distinctly noisy since the end of the steam age. Also, of course, there is now a lot more town between what was the Rushden of then, and Irchester.

Higham Feast was always the second Sunday of August, and the adage for that was, "Higham feast, shut your doors, Rushden feast, light your fires." Rushden feast was then, as now, the Sunday following the 19th September. Bearing these dates in mind, it made absolute sense to adhere to these customs.

Rushden feast, I was given to understand by, "Buggy," my history teacher, was to commemorate the founding of St. Mary's' church. It was also a convenient fair for the contracting of labour for the ensuing years.

All this was forgotten by my contemporaries and myself, in the excitement generated by the arrival of the fair, which was always referred to as, "The Feast."

"The feast's here!" went up the cry, and everyone found an excuse to pass Spencer Park on their way home from school. Even luckier were they, who actually saw the arrival of Charles Thurston's massive transporters, towed by steam traction engines, all in a very attractive livery of maroon and gold, with gleaming brassware all over.

Had we never got to the fair itself, the arrival was enough to send us into transports of delight.

On the Thursday of 'Feast week', we were given a half holiday from school, and anyone who was able to save some money for that occasion was rich indeed, as all the rides were at half price. In addition to this, it was considered by many to be a town holiday, and a lot of parents, on at least one occasion, indulged their children.

I am aware, as I write this, that Rushden feast is still celebrated with a fair, but the way it differs is that it is not so much the attraction of the year now, it is merely one more amusement in a long run of amusements that people enjoy, (or endure), through the year.

Out of our meagre exchequer of a few pennies we would indulge in a "feast ball", some, "mint candy" that we had watched being made, a toffee apple, a blower that trilled, and with an enormous amount of luck, possibly a coconut.

The luck factor would be on the "Rolling pennies", which, if you won, paid out your stake of one penny, and a chance to win again. The player who was both lucky and careful could amass sixpence, and afford a coconut.

I have written elsewhere about Tommy Essam and his prizes that last a lifetime, but there are other names worthy of noting. The darts stall was run by a family called Sumners, or Summers, and the sweetmeats were made by Tilleys of Kettering. Outside the fairground was 'The Crockery King', who would sell half dinner services at the rate of about one every two minutes. It was fascinating to see him seemingly to juggle with the crockery and smash it all together, without doing the slightest damage to it, talking all the time, and selling everything he picked up from his vast stocks.

There were also specialist attractions within the fair which were not rides, nor sales, but legitimate entertainment.

The "Wall of death", and the Boxing booth, where all comers were challenged to three rounds with the "Champ".

I think it is true to say the Rushden Feast is not what it once was.

Charles Thurston "Golden Peacocks" ride 1929

RUSHDEN HIGH ST. IN THE THIRTIES

Let us take a stroll along Rushden High Street, starting from the railway station end. We can call at the first shop, Jessie Robinsons', for a newspaper, or perhaps a book from her lending library.

We may want to arrange out portrait, or wedding photos taken by Mr. Edgar Linnet at the next shop. Smart, the butcher/poulterer will be pleased to supply us with our requirements for tomorrows lunch, and we call at Walpole Smiths for bread and cakes or buns for tea.

If we have enough room in our basket, we may wish to pop in to Roe Bros. For some item of haberdashery, before crossing Victoria Road to Billy Keller, the greengrocer.

Elsie Butlin is almost always a port of call for most ladies, because there it is that knitting wool, and patterns, may be purchased. Radio is coming into its most popular era, in the late thirties, and where better to buy your new Phillips or Marconi, than Clark Bros.

Some people prefer cakes by Barlows to Walpoles. Here is the opportunity to get them, before looking at the latest cookers in the showroom of "The Rushden and Higham Ferrers Gas Light and Coke Co."

Set up high upon the top of a stone wall, is the farmhouse and yard belonging to Marriotts. It has not yet been demolished to make way for the very modern shops, with flats over, that are to be occupied by Mr. Swartz, Optician, the owner of the only public clock other than the church, in Rushden. (The one on the front of the General post office doesn't work). The other shops in the group remain empty, due, probably to the imminence of war.

The next rather large establishment is Phillips, whose main trade is in soft furnishings, bedding, curtains and so on, but they will be pleaes to sell you a card of shirt buttons, if that is what you need.

Close by Phillips, if not next door, is the shop of Hedley, the chemist, and next door to Hedleys is a High class confectioners known as, "The Chocolate Box". Not only do they sell top brand sweets, this is the place to buy such things as almond icing, candied peel, and all those special things that go to make a Christmas cake.

At the foot of Woburn Place (Sounds a bit 'grand' doesn't it, but its only an alley) is a seedman/florist named Seckington, and a fruit shop which is run by someone called Clark. And then just across the other side of the alley, which is only a stepped path wide, is the shoe shop of Wm. Timpson.

Now we are coming into the really busy part of the street, where all the shoppers congregate. But let us carry on walking in the same direction and on the same side and we can walk back along the other side when we get to the church. (There are numerous churches in Rushden, but only St. Mary's is referred to as 'The Church')

Here we have the stationers, Croft and Nichols, Pork butcher Billy Russel, Meadows the Gents hairdresser, Eastman's the butcher, and right on the corner of Queen St. An old type grocery, old fashioned even in the thirties, Battersbys. Here it is that you can buy all your dried fruit, peas, beans, and so forth, from the sack, or in the case of fruit, from the block.

Across the other side of Queen street is one of the more modern grocers, The Star Supply Stores, followed by "The Louvre", and "The Bon Marche". French names for businesses are very 'in' at this time. Liptons of tea fame, comes next, and although they were originally tea importers, you can now buy any item of fresh grocery here.

Right in the centre spot in the High Street, stands the Wesleyan Chapel, and very near here, not necessarily in this order, are Burtons the grocer, (whose cheese inspired a parody of a popular song in the trenches), then Hals the draper, Wanklyns the jeweller, (the same shop as is a jewellers in the nineties,) Willmott, a farm produce and dairy shop, from a farm in the town, and a large area of shop which houses the CO-OP millinery and corsetry, etc. Departments.

Next is the old Succouth Chapel, which is fast falling into a state of disrepair, and Gramshaws furnishing, then, on the corner of George Street, is the shop of Horace Wills, Radios and Records filled on Saturday afternoons with teenagers browsing through the catalogues of Columbia, Brunswick, Parlophone, Regal Zonophone H.M.V. and any other that came to hand. How many records are sold I have no idea, but as a venue on a cold winter afternoon it takes some beating. No wonder it is called "The Sound Stores".

The next block includes, "The House of Fashion", Blunts, another material store, another optician whose name may well be Mr. Swartz, a confectioner, and Webbs, the gentlemen's outfitters. These are all in a block known as "Cleavers Chambers". In these same premises are the chambers of the local law firm of Parker and Groome, Commisioners for Oaths, whatever that might mean! But it sounds good.

Knights the jeweller, and Knights the Furnisher, take us to Coffee Tavern Lane, which is called after the real coffee tavern that occupies the site opposite. This is truly Rushden's "Pub with no beer", being a "Temperance Hotel".

Do you need a new piano? Or a block of resin for your violin bow? Or a string for your ukelele? Fraser Son and McKenzie is the place to get them. But if you need some work done to your property, your tradesman will call next door to H.P.Hodge, the builders and plumbers merchant, (Fireplaces a speciality) to pick up his supplies.

Warren the butcher is nex, followed by Horsleys, the pet store, before coming to Wills' fashion shop at the corner of Newton Road. This part of the High St, is still known as Wards Corner because a shop of that name once occupied what is now Wills'.

We are now at the very beginning of the High Street and are facing a very narrow bit of road in front of the church. There's talk of widening it some day. While we are here, lets just cross over the road and see the shops in Church Parade.

Right next to the green is the hairdresser, Jim Knight. He is also the tobacconist, and the angling store, and the gossip shop for all the towns businessmen. There are probably more deals done here than over any office desk. It is the thirties equivalent of the golfing weekend, to go for a shave at Jim Knight's.

Coming northwards now, we get to the Lightstrung Bicycle Co. Looked after by old Frank Tassel. The Lightstrung Co. Has moved to the premises which were once the Gas Company at the corner of Duck Street and instead of cycles, they now deal in Morris cars. You can buy a Morris eight for £100, but petrol is expensive at 11d per gallon.

Frank still loves and sells bikes.

Next to Frank Tassel is the furnisher and supplier of prams, J.H. Taylor, Ada will probably be able to tell you the date of the happy event better than you can tel her. The little ironmongers shop next along, is almost lost among the more imposing portals of its neighbours, but if you want a garden spade, you could go to see the Fairey Bros. Whose shop it is. (When the Fairey brothers retire the little shop will be taken on by a young man called Peter Crisp, I wonder if he'll make a go of it?)

Fleemans the chemist, is the shop on the corner, and maintains a good trade by, among other things, being on route from most of the doctors whose surgeries are in Park Road, and the bonus of having a bus stop just outside the door.

The High street proper starts with the next shop, Charles Robinson's Newsagents and fancy goods. This is the premier newsagents of the town, employing seemingly scores of paperboys for morning delivery. Close to, if not next door, is an establishment run by Florrie Gross, which could loosely be described as a milliners, but which also sells art materials, and needlework patterns and silks. Hereabouts, too, is Abingtons, Gents Tailors, and Boots the Chemist, on the site which it will occupy for at least another fifty years.

The thing that always strikes me about Boots is that it only sells medicinal things, and soap, and even the soap smells medicinal.

Sitting over the top of Boots is a place I hate to visit, but find it very necessary to do so. I refer to Messrs North and Neave, dentists. Mr. North, who is my dentist, was trained by a slap happy butcher, who practised on dead soldiers. That at least, is my theory. I might not have run foul of him had I only avoided the next shops, Wrights confectionery, and Cookes Ice Cream shop.

Flavell Hart, outfitters, The National Provincial Bank, The Countryside library, and Seabrooks greengrocery, stand cheek by jowl with Freeman Hardy and Willis, and the CO-OP men's outfitters. (A made to measure suit for less than a fiver). After which comes Webbs, Saddlery and leather goods.

"HOME AND COLONIAL"... now doesn't that conjure up some thoughts of empire? Not that I approve of empires in particular, but when a large part of the globe is covered with red hatching, there is a feeling of certainty, and permanence.

Home and Colonial is only a grocers, but I think their boast is that everything they sell is produced in the British Empire. It is an easy boast, seeing that most of the world is British Colonies.

Nevilles, tobacconist, travel agent, stationer, etc. etc. will still be in the same spot fifty years hence. Run by the same family, selling the same services, that it did when it was first started. What an achievement.

The Palace Cinema, the entrance of which is next door, was never a High Street cinema, but it likes to pretend that it is, so we can leave it in that position and call at yet another Gramshaw furnishers, of which there are three in the town.

The office of the Evening Telegraph may or may not have always been there, but at the time of our walk, it is. Next door to it is Saxbys pork butchers, (a mere branch of the Wellingborough based firm) and a confectioners shop which has the appearance of having seen better days, with confections to match.

In juxtaposition to these is an office, and in the office, when he is not working, is a man of whom it has been said, "He never sleeps." Not much of a recommendation for the business head and sole proprietor of 'Maxis taxis'.

Just before we come to the 'Rose and Crown', there is a little shop in the name of 'Dunkley', another hairdresser/tobacconist and stationer. destined to last another fifty years.

If we could be on this corner on Saturday we could buy a 'Football Telegraph' from Freddy Hales and stand and listen to the Salvation Army Band before crossing over to the General Post Office, one of the more imposing buildings in the town.

Hootons penny Bazaar is next, and then Pooles, a high class toy shop and pram centre. Bikes and radios are sold next door at Currys, and a fruit shop and a wallpaper shop immediately precede Woolworths.

Part of the Woolworths building is occupied by a dairy shop called "The Maypole." Lots of people only patronise this shop to purchase Maypole butter, and buy the rest of their groceries elsewhere.

There is a small gap or drive, separating Woolworths from a detached shop, a fruiterers called the Quick Turnover. It is run by the family

Fett, and retains it's name when taken over by the Jones family.

"The Feathers" is a shiny new pub, built on the site of the old one of the same name, and within the same block is the very latest fashion house. "Roses Fashion Centre". it is made to look ever more modern by being adjacent to some of the long established businesses.

In its white tiled shop premises is the LONDON CENTRAL MEAT CO. Ltd. And next to that is the pawn shop of Brooke and Brooke. Hopes, the pork butchers is next, presided over by Mrs Illiffe, whose family are to establish themselves in businesses all over town. It is here that Jim Bugby, Fishmonger and poulterer, runs his business from an open fronted shop, and will one day hand it over to Jim Jnr, who will run it until he, himself, retires.

Now we are at Rollie Cox's Fish restaurant, and one more shop. Wrights babywear, brings us to West St. At the other side of West St. Is Haigh's furniture store, who specialise in carpets that according to their own advert, "Can't be beaten". The electricity showroom is next, and the grocery of Tailby and Putnam, these are grocers to the well to do of the town, and are the only licensed grocer to the best of my recollection. Here it is that bacon is sliced from the joint chosen by the customer, on one of those clever machines that will one day be commonplace, but at this time are a rarity. Here. Mr. Turner will pat up a pound of dairy butter by hand, with the use of butter pats, as you want it- and finish it with a motif when it is ready.

Alf Gray, the Ironmonger is next, and he will weigh out a pound of nails for you, and wrap them in brown paper, for a couple of pence. Lloyds Bank and a cottage brings us to "Puns Lane" (restricted for heavy traffic over two tons) and across the road to Bates fish shop. Bates fish shop is a many-faceted affair. In the morning they sell wet fish, and in the evening they sell fish and chips, as do most of the other fish shops in town, but at Bates, in the evening particularly Saturday evening, ordinary working class people can afford to go for a meal of fish and chips with peas, bread and butter and a cup of tea, served in a very few minutes, for sixpence. (Two and a Half New pence)

Leaving the supper room of Bates fish shop we may, if we wish, call for a drink next door at the Railway Inn, before walking the last few yards along the main artery of our very busy town. We pass the 'Belgian House', so called because it housed Belgian refugees during the great war, and we look into the window of Joe Page, bespoke tailor.

At this point, we could cross the road and start the journey over again, if we were in our teens, and it was a Saturday evening, that is precisely what we would be doing, several times over. Known by all as "the Bunny Run". This half mile of Rushden was one of the main meeting places for many life partnerships.

WALKING AROUND THE EDGES

There is one thing that constanly amazes me as I look back fifty or sixty years, and that is the amount of walking we used to do. It's true there was a bus service, and the fare from the church to Irchester Road was only one penny, but we walked and saved the penny. But that is only by the way.

My family or my dad's family to be more accurate, lived around the town, and I mean around, not in, and whenever we visited them it meant a long walk. For example, Aunt Win' lived at Chelveston, Aunt Elsie lived at Sanders Lodge, Uncle Claude at Higham Ferrers, and we walked to see them. I can distinctly remember a visit to Chelveston, and I must only have been a toddler, because I had my, "Pusher" with us. I was a nuisance, because I insisted on walking and helping to push, I suppose for about a hundred yards, and then I would want to be pushed. We travelled by this method from our home in Irchester Road to Chelveston (about three miles) had tea, and then travelled back. I remember the debate on whether or not we should catch a bus from Higham to Rushden, but it was decided we would be "nearly home" before the bus was due. So we walked.

We had some family friends, the Faireys, who lived at the top of the hill in Newton road. The house was built on a smallholding, with orchards, pigsties, chickens, Etc. And water from a well. It was a marvellous place for a small boy to visit. And visit we did. We walked.

I would spend the time there playing in the hay, and running in the orchards and all those other lovely things one can do on a miniature farm. And when I was fit to drop, the call would come for me to walk home, two miles at least.

If we didn't go visiting anyone on Sunday, the evening was a time to walk the edges. This was something like, "Beating the Bounds", but in Rushden it was, "A walk round the edges". Our own particular edge was from the Rushden/Knuston border in Irchester Road, and started at Pig Lane. From here we could head for Ditchford Lane, and at that junction, turn right towards Higham (Thompsons, the butchers) and come back over the hill to Washbrook Road and home.

Alternatively, we could go from the same point and head in the opposite direction, by the gardenfield, and Downings feld, and the mushroom field, and the Hilly Holly field, and the newt pond into

Wymington Road near to the Mill estate, thence down Wymington Road, High Street South, Wellingborough Road and home.

Other Rushdeners had different edges to walk. My wife's family for instance, lived at the junction of Cromwell Road and Smarts Road (Hayden Road) so their "Edges" would be up Smarts Road and via the many fields to finish at what is now the Toll Bar. This one was exciting because it involved crossing the single line railway track between Rushden and Higham.

There was a less well-defined walk from Newton Road via Bedford Road to Wymington. I only remember the tangent green lane from the isolation hospital, (used for the Scarlet fever epidemics) in Bedford Road to Link Road. Fewer people beat these bounds, because fewer people lived there.

We still have remnants, in name, of these walks, (which were truly country walks then,) in Boundary Avenue and the misnamed The Hedges. As the town has grown in size, in fact so much that it now actually reaches the edges in most cases, and in population, it seems to have diminished in status.

WHERE IS RUSHDEN

I don't know if you've noticed, as I have, that Rushden as far as the weather goes, just doesn't have any. None of it's own that is. When Michael Fish or David Brooks, or whoever, draws lines on the map of Britain, whether it be from the Bristol Channel to The Wash, or from London to Liverpool, of from The Channel Islands to Shetland, it is always a bit curved, and it always cuts through Rushden High St.

The westher on one side of the line may be wet and windy, and on the other side bright and sunny, but we never know which side we are on. We just know that we'll just get the edge of someone else's weather. It is the same story when you try to use a road map. Whatever page you open the map at (or unfold it if it's that type) Rushden will either be just under the staple in the centre crease, or right at the edge of the page, with all the road you want on the next map, which is 10 pages away.

It isn't all bad news, however. We can choose to be, West or East Anglia or East Midlands or North of the Home Countis, or South of the North/South divide.

Long ago, when I was a coalman, and coal was rationed. Rushden was in the North, and a ration of 50 hundredweights per year was allowed, but in Wymington, which actually joined Rushden and was only 1 mile from the station anyway, the ration was only 30 hundredweights, because they were in the south. Once more, the powers that be had drawn a line on the map, (or had gone up to the crease). I can assure everyone that Wymington, in midwinter, is every bit as cold as Rushden.

The great thing is that Rushden is not only right in the centre of England, it is in the centre of the universe. The same distance applies whether you travel around the world in an easterly, or in a westerly direction. Or for that matter, if you shoot up the Greenwich Meridian, over the North pole, down the International date line, and back up line '0' again. And we all know that Earth is the centre of the universe, don't we? All that being the case. Why isn't Rushden the Capital?

THE TANK

As far as I am aware, Rushden has no statues of any of its great men or women, perhaps because it never had any, or perhaps, if it did, they were not known to be great. Arguably, Billy Capon, John Spencer, H.E.Bates and the Denton twins could be so honoured. No? Oh well, perhaps not!

In the absence of statues, our town had just two monuments. The cenotaph was at one end of the town, set in it's well kept garden, opposite the church of St. Mary, and at ther other end of the town, in Spencer Park, was a relic of the Great War of 1914 – 1918, in the shape of a tank. Disembowelled, but real.

Although the war had not been over very long, historically speaking, to we boys the tank was something historical, like stocks, or castle ruins, and similar things found in many towns. It was not revered in any way, but was looked on merely as another toy, or one more piece of equipment on which to climb and slide, and ruin ones trousers.

Mr. and Mrs. Surridge in their Model "T" outside their house in Brookfield Road. Note the iron railings, a feature of most houses in Rushden before the War.

Although to the people who fought, and survived that unholy conflict, the tank had a special significance, this piece of equipment was taken

from us at the commencement of the second bit of unpleasantness. Mainly, we have since been told, as a bit of tub-thumping propaganda, along with the characteristic cast iron railings which were a feature of the mainly Victorian houses in the town.

I imagine that thescrapyard that was just across the road from where the tank was sited, contained about as much scrap at the end of the war as was collected by this exercise, but it made people feel good to make this sacrifice. It seems strange, and wrong, that the field pieces of earlier wars are still intact on the Thames embankment, as is the armour in the Tower of London.

Rushden's monument to the futility of war was only one of a number of things that have been eroded from our municipal life. Spencer Park was once a park for children. In it were three sets of swings, boys, girls and infants. There were two Jazzes, and a Bumper. There were bars of varying height, a Maypole and for the young men to show off their prowess, a set of swinging rings, hanging from a frame, from which they could swing, Tarzan like, hand over hand, end to end.

There was also a bandstand, which was often occupied by one of the towns four brass bands. And, of course there was another one in the Hall Park. The brook was not fenced in, and there were at least three bridges over it. In all Spencer Park was a very pleasant place to be.

In summer, the paddling pool was always full, both with water, and with mother-accompanied children enjoying it. The Putting greens, the Bowling greens, and grass Tennis courts were in constant use throughout the season, but nothing was in use on Sunday.

I remember Spencer Park as being clean, and well-ordered and well kept. Of course, with a bit of expenditure, and a lot of thought, and a lot of care, it could be again.

But the tank; Well that piece of history, as they say, is History!

AND IN CONCLUSION

I remember fondly, the Rushden of my youth. I hate it when the good things I recall are just left to fade away, or are destroyed in some way or another. My pet hate is vandalism, whether by yobs, or by the authorities.

I feel that I am reasonably progressive in my thinking, and I like a lot of the changes that have taken place since the war finished. In fifty years, these are many, and so there should be. Not all are good.

I dislike the approaches to Rushden from Wellingborough being disfigured by those awful warehouse monstrosities on the Sanders Lodge/Northampton Road Development, I like, however, the tasteful building that is Hamblin's garage, in the same area.

What is wrong with the warehouses is not the design of the buildings, but the fact they can be seen for literally miles, in a green fields area. Nearer to the town would have been more acceptable, and a sight more convenient to those who work in them, I would have thought.

The housing developments around and within the town, including some of the council sponsored estates, show some exciting examples of architecture and good taste, unlike the row upon row of terraced houses that are a feature of the earlier parts of the town.

I particularly like the Hamblin Court area between High Street and Rectory Road, and also the use of factory sites in the building of flats for sale and for rent. Using them as factories would have been better, but we can't have everything, can we?

As I write, a much needed shopping centre is being built on the old CO -OP hall site in the High Street. I wish it all success. May the residents of the town use and appreciate what they have.

I would like to see a return to the system of town councils, instead of representation on a much larger body, that seems so remote that we no longer feel like a town.

I would like to see our public parks and areas financed and supported by a local body. A body where the members are the same folks who walk in the parks, who see the scars, and who see the potential, and have the power to do something.

Parks, I know, have always been the "Cinderella" service in local government. But parks make a town worth visiting, or not, as the case may be.

I commend to councillors, particularly those members of the parks committee, St. Neots, where a previously marshy waste was turned into a major tourist attraction. I commend to them Leamington Spa. Whose town centre gardens attract thousands of visitors each year. In Nuneaton, a town not unlike our own, the best possible use is made of the brook no bigger that our Washbrook, landscaping it through the park in the centre of town.

It all needs money of course, but so does every venture that is worthwhile. The thing about an attractive town is just that, it is attractive, and it brings trade in. Perhaps this is a problem to be mulled over by the "Chamber of Trade", rather than the local authority.

A strong campaign against litter, particularly in the main shopping area, is a must. Off street parking in areas which are at the moment restricted in space would be great, but expensive. Perhaps a few Cul De Sacs in what are now short side streets would ease the traffic danger. This has been done in Bedford in some parts with what appears to be great success.

Unless someone kidnaps me and carries me off, I will live in Rushden until I die. I would like to live in a place that is at least as good as it was when I came into the world. Better if possible.

DITCHFORD MILL

The other day I chanced to see
A place, which when I was but three,
I visited with Mum and Dad,
And what a lovely time we had.

Clear flowed the stream o'er gravel bed
The spit of sand, where fathers led
His child to catch some sticklebacks
And redthroats letting mum relax,

And chat with other mothers there
Forgetting all their weekly care
Whilst sitting in the June sunshine
Regaled with tales of 'Treacle Mine',

But what a change I see here now,
A sweeter scent comes from a sow
Environed in her stinking sty,
Who never sees an open sky

Foul putrification is the smell
Man making profits makes manmade hell
Litters of lorries are disembowelled,
The stream is with the contents fouled,
Whilst noisome fumes hang in a pall,
Oh! How I longed to end it all.

Our Poet Laureate, forgiven now
Said, 'Come, friendly bombs, and fall on slough'
And, having smelled this odious scent
I realise just what he meant.

Cottages and workshops in Duck Street, not too long before demolition